Frankenstein

Mary Shelley

Adapted and simplified by John Turvey

Illustrated by Hugh Marshall

Longman

1200 word
vocabulary

Chapter One

I do not know whether this story ought to be told. In some ways, I think it should not. It is so strange that some readers may not believe it; and to them, at least, it can do no harm. But it is just possible that a few will believe it, and might be drawn into the dark and secret ways that my friend followed. And I do not wish to be the cause of such an evil. To anyone who chooses to get mixed up in such matters, and hopes to escape the pain and horror that my friend suffered, I can only say this: you have been warned!

The truth is that I am an old man now, and of the four who once knew the whole unhappy story I am the only one still alive. I do not wish the story to die with me. For mixed with the horror is the story of the life and death of a great man — and this should not be forgotten.

But it is time to say something about myself. My name is Henri Clerval, and I was born in the city of Geneva in the year 1775, the son of a cloth merchant. I was an only child, and this for me was the cause of much unhappiness. If I had had a brother he might have learned my father's trade, and in the end have taken over my father's business. As it was, I was expected to do this. From my earliest years this was what my father planned for me. But I was not interested in the business — or, indeed, in any business. I tried. I wanted to please him. But the shop was for me like a desert. I took my pleasure not in getting money but from reading books; and as I grew older we quarrelled. My mother had died when I was very young, and there was no one to make peace between us. Thus life at home became unhappy, and would have become impossible if I had not had Victor Frankenstein as a friend.

The Frankensteins were also a merchant family, but richer and more important than us Clervals. They had been active in the government of the city for a hundred years. Because they were rich they did not have to give all their time to trade: they were interested in the arts and in science — most of all science. They were restless people with restless, questioning minds. Like most of his family, my friend's father had travelled widely, and after making a late marriage had lived some years in Italy.

I still remember my first visit to their house in the Rue des Granges, the street where the oldest and richest families in Geneva lived. The old Italian pictures on the walls acted strongly on my young mind. How different, I thought, was our house in the lower part of the town. It was then that Frankenstein told me that he had been born in Italy.

As we stood talking in the hall, a rather pretty girl, perhaps a year younger than us, walked through and smiled as she passed.

'That is my sister,' he said. 'She was also born in Italy. She is, in fact, Italian.'

I did not understand. How could she be Italian when his parents were Swiss?

'Of course, she is not really my sister,' he said, 'but we have been brought up together, and we think of each other as brother and sister. Let me tell you how it happened.

'One day my parents were walking along the shore of one of the Italian lakes north of Milan, where they were living at that time. The day was warm, and, feeling thirsty, they stopped at a small farm for something to drink. It was a poor place, but even the poorest house in those parts could supply a little milk or wine.

'The farmer's wife took them into the kitchen, where they saw five little heads round the table with a cup of soup in front of each. But while four of the little heads were dark, the fifth was fair, and looked quite different from the parents. My mother was curious and asked the woman about her. The woman told an interesting story.

'The child was not hers but the daughter of a landowner of that place who had lost his life trying to free his country from an unjust government. The mother had died earlier. The father, before his death, had placed the child in the care of the farmer's wife, who had looked after her when she was a baby. The father's lands had been taken by the government after his death, and since there were no other members of the family, the child had stayed with them.

'My parents were interested in this story. My mother was not strong. It was not certain then that she would have another child. So, not having a daughter of her own, she asked the farmer and his wife if she could take the child and bring her up as her own.

'The farmer and his wife did not want to give her up, but they knew that they could never offer her as much as my parents, who must have seemed very rich to them. So it was arranged, with the help of the village authorities, that Elizabeth Lavenza, as she was called, became a Frankenstein.' He smiled. 'A pretty story, is it not?'

'Like something from a book,' I replied. 'You are lucky to have a sister. I have no one to talk to at home.'

Frankenstein smiled again. 'Then she must become your sister, too.' I do not know why he suddenly said that. But his words came true. She did become a sister to me, and remained a sister all the time that we were children. All three of us belonged to each other. Even now I feel we still belong to each other, and always will.

Chapter Two

I soon learned more about the Frankensteins. After
Elizabeth joined the family they gave up their wandering
life and returned to settle in Geneva — or, to be exact,
near Geneva, because although they had this fine house
in the town, where Victor and Elizabeth lived when
they had to go to school, they also had a house in the
country. This was six kilometres beyond the town on
the south side of the lake looking over the Jura mountains.
The Frankensteins liked it better there. They did not mind
a quiet life, and being a close and happy family they did
not seem to feel the need for company.

In this Victor was like his parents. At school he had
few friends, and of these I was the closest. This made me
feel proud since even at the age when I first knew him he
appeared a person of unusual powers of mind. However,
he was not always easy to be with. Sometimes the
strength of his feelings made him angry; and his long,
strange silences were even less easy to bear. But I thought
more of him than any other person I knew — except, of
course, for Elizabeth, whose sweetness delighted all who
knew her. The friendly feelings between Victor, Elizabeth,
and myself were so perfect that even then it seemed to
me that they could only be ended by death.

These were happy years, and for the Frankensteins
happiness seemed complete with the birth of another son.
He was called William; and with him arrived Justine, a
happy country girl of our age who came to look after
him. This was the circle of people among whom I passed
my young days.

From the beginning Frankenstein's interests lay in
science. He studied nature with a kind of hunger, seeing
the world around him as if it was so many secrets to be
discovered. Living where we did, there were secrets

enough for those who wanted to see: in the blue waters
of the lake, which went down three hundred metres; in
the glaciers — the great rivers of ice that flowed down
from the mountains; in the mountains themselves, and
in the changes of weather and season. There was so much
to excite scientific curiosity.

But strangely enough it was in Frankenstein's nature
to be drawn to a different kind of science from the one
that is studied in our universities. I well remember one
summer when we were spending a few days at Thonon,
a town in Savoy further along on the south side of the
lake. The weather had turned wet and we could not go
out. In a little room under the roof Frankenstein found
a dusty old book that promised to unlock the secrets of
nature. To me it looked more like magic than science,
but Frankenstein was so interested in it that he could not
put it down. For the next two years it was his daily
study and the cause of all his experiments.

This interest in magic and secret knowledge remained
with Frankenstein all through his schooldays. Nor did it
ever completely leave him. He did not then know the
orderly ways of modern science, but when he did in
later life, I think he found them too slow for him. He
always wanted quick results.

Elizabeth and I were not interested in the same things
as Frankenstein. We used to like writing little pieces to
be acted, and we would all act in them, including
William and Justine. But we also enjoyed helping
Frankenstein with his experiments. Even then he was
interested in the nature of life itself. He was trying to
find what so many students of old times had failed to
find — the magic liquid that was supposed to make man
live for ever.

But did Frankenstein want to live for ever?

'Is that what you really want?' asked Elizabeth one

day as all four of us were standing round, watching him
set up another of his experiments. He looked surprised.
I do not think he had ever seriously thought about it.

'No,' he said after a minute's thought. 'At least,
I wouldn't like to live for ever by myself. I would not
like to be alone. You would have to live for ever, too —
all of you.' He looked round smiling, and his eyes rested
on Justine's face.

'I should like that,' she said simply. Between her and
Frankenstein I often noticed at that time a feeling of
warmth and understanding. It was not surprising that
she was his most trusted helper in his work-room.

However, one day — we must have been about fourteen
at the time — something happened which in the end helped
to turn Frankenstein's studies away from magic and
towards modern science.

It was one of those summer days when the hot, dry
wind from the south brings unsettled weather.
Frankenstein and I had been out since early morning on
the Salève, the long, low mountain whose white cliffs
can be seen from every part of Geneva. We had been
collecting wild plants for Frankenstein's experiments,
and felt hot and tired. Luckily we had already come
down from the mountain, and were making our way
across a field with a line of fruit trees on one side, when
a thunderstorm broke. Although we were getting very
wet we decided not to stand under the trees because the
flashes of lightning seemed all too close, and we knew
how dangerous it was.

Suddenly there was a noise like a gun going off, and
at the same time a flash of blue light — then darkness, as
we lay on the ground blinded by the flash and unable to
hear from the noise. It was as if a great wind had blown
us down. A few minutes later, though still hardly able to
think, we could at least see and hear again. We got up

from the wet grass and saw nearby the remains of a tree, black and smoking.

It had been struck by lightning.

All this would have left an unforgettable picture in anyone's mind. I certainly remember everything most clearly. But for Frankenstein it was something more. It was almost as if it had changed his life. The power of lightning was something that he could never forget, and from that day, I think, a certain idea began to form in his mind.

From that day also he seemed to lose interest in the magical ideas that had meant so much to him up to this time, even if he did not at once take up the study of modern science. For two years he gave himself completely to the science of numbers; not, I think now, because ordinary science did not interest him, but because it interested him too much. He was afraid of the power which science put into the hands of these who studied it. He was afraid of the use to which he himself might put those powers.

Chapter Three

When Frankenstein reached the age of seventeen his father decided to send him to the university of Ingolstadt in Germany. He could have kept his son at his studies in Geneva, but he had a friend, a Dr Krempe, who taught at Ingolstadt, and many people spoke well of his teaching. Besides, old Frankenstein believed it was good for a young man to study away from home and to get used to the ways of other countries.

However, before Frankenstein could leave for Ingolstadt something happened which caused him and all of us the deepest sorrow. First Elizabeth fell ill. Then his mother, in looking after her, caught her illness. Elizabeth got better, but Victor's mother, who had never been strong, did not. It soon became clear that she was not going to live. While she still had the strength to speak, she called Victor and Elizabeth to her bedside. Joining their hands together, she said:

'Victor, my dear, I had hoped that I would live to see you and Elizabeth married. It is my dearest wish that your father will live to see it.'

Then, asking Elizabeth to come closer, she said:
'Elizabeth, you must now be mother to my William.'
She died soon after.

After a few weeks Frankenstein went off to Ingolstadt at last, leaving an unhappy family behind him. For Elizabeth, at least, there was much to do. The care of the family had become her duty and to be busy was the best escape from unhappiness. William still had Elizabeth and Justine. But it was hard for old Frankenstein. His was the heaviest loss to bear.

I, too, felt sad: sad at the death of a woman who had always been a second mother to me, sad at the going away of my closest friend, and sad also because I could not continue my own studies. My father would not listen to me when I asked to go to university. Buying and selling were for him the only important things in life, and he could only see laziness, and too much drinking and spending in the student way of life. I tried to change his way of thinking, but he was not to be moved, and I went into my father's shop.

All the same, I did not give up all hope of further study. I kept the hope alive by reading the letters which Frankenstein sent me — letters which showed that getting to a university was not the end of life's difficulties: only the beginning of new ones.

I did not see Frankenstein again for two years. Nor did his family. We all received letters from him at first, but towards the end of his first year these became fewer and shorter and told us less. Was this because he had less news to tell? Certainly he seemed to be giving all his time to his work. But what was this work? It did not seem to be part of his ordinary university studies. I began to think he did not want to say too much about it.

At least we learned something about his first few months at the university. Surprising as it may seem, he had gone to Ingolstadt without any fixed idea of what to study. It was more by chance than his father's being friendly with Dr Krempe that he joined the classes of the two men who taught science. I think he still thought science was a dangerous game which he did not quite dare to play.

Hans Krempe was a short, heavy man with unbrushed hair and beard. His face was ugly and his manners were rough. But he was a good scientist and a strong-minded teacher. He had no doubt that Frankenstein ought to study science, and told him so. He asked him if he had ever studied the subject before. When he heard of my friend's early studies in magic he cried out in horror.

'Did you really spend so many years in studying such stuff? Every minute you have spent on those books has been completely wasted. Where have you been living? Was there nobody in Geneva kind enough to point out to you the worthlessness of these fairy stories? I cannot understand your good father allowing this. My dear young man, you must begin your studies again from the beginning.'

He then wrote down a list of books which he asked Frankenstein to buy, and said that he would begin giving his classes that week — on three mornings a week. 'On the other three days Dr Waldman will take classes. We must lead you out of Fairyland, where you have been living too long.'

Peter Waldman, the other teacher, was a very different kind of man, younger, small and well dressed. His voice was sweet, and he spoke with seriousness about his subject. His first talk moved my friend's feelings deeply, and he wrote down this man's words in one of the first letters he sent from Ingolstadt.

'The teachers of this science in older times,' Waldman said, 'promised impossibilities, and in the end could offer nothing. The modern teacher promises little: he knows that one metal cannot be changed into another, and that it is useless to seek the magic liquid that gives everlasting life. But he does have wonderful things to show. The laws of nature are being uncovered. The heights of the air, the deepest parts of the sea and land, the human body itself—all these are giving up their secrets one by one.'

He went on to give such a picture of the forward movement of science and the place of the scientist in modern life that Frankenstein decided, then and there, that this was to be his study.

He was so excited that he hardly slept that night. The next morning he called on Dr Waldman and found him friendly and helpful. He listened seriously when Frankenstein told him about his earlier scientific studies and did not laugh, as Professor Krempe had done.

'We owe these writers much,' he said. 'All science builds on the discoveries of earlier times. You seem to have begun your studies young. You may yourself make discoveries. One day, perhaps, you will surprise us.'

Chapter Four

So Frankenstein returned to science, even if it was different from the science he had begun to follow as a boy. His later letters told a story of one success after

another. From Krempe he learned much about the making of experiments, while from Waldman he continued to receive much kindness. From both he quickly learned the little that was to be learned about the subject in those days.

In the rooms he had taken at the top of a tall, old house near the university he built his own work-room, and very soon he was spending most of his time there. The stars sometimes disappeared in the light of the morning before he stopped work and went to bed.

As I have said, Frankenstein wrote quite often during his first year at Ingolstadt. But about September of the following year his letters stopped. He did not come home to Geneva for holidays, and I could see that his father and Elizabeth were troubled. In his last letter he said that he had learned as much as Ingolstadt could teach him. If this was true, what was it that still kept him there? Even a letter to Krempe brought a reply that added little to what they knew. Frankenstein had indeed left the university — against Krempe's wishes — and was now following some studies of his own (though what these studies were, Krempe did not say).

Eight months passed without any news, and then old Frankenstein decided to act.

'Somebody must go to Ingolstadt. It cannot be me. My travelling days are over, and Elizabeth cannot give up her duties in the house. We shall have to arrange something,' he said, giving me a look full of meaning.

Soon after this, old Frankenstein appeared at my house and asked to see my father. My father, as I have said, was a hard man, but old Frankenstein was good at making people change their ideas. The fact that he was rich and an important man also helped my father to allow the following arrangement to take place. In return for help with the cost of my studies I would go to Ingolstadt,

where I would enter the university and find out what Victor was doing. Having found out, I was to look after him if necessary, and to make him write home.

So it happened that because my friend stopped writing letters I was able to escape from my father's shop and do what I wanted to do above all things — to go to university.

The very next day I took the public carriage from Geneva to Lausanne and from there to Berne. It was a four day journey across Switzerland to Lake Constance, then into South Germany by Ulm to Ingolstadt.

It was late afternoon when the carriage crossed the River Danube and entered the walls of that pleasant old town, then washed in the golden light of late summer. That, at least, is how it must have appeared to me that first time. But when I think of what happened later — when I think of what first saw the light in that little town, I cannot remember Ingolstadt without feelings of pain and horror.

I left my bags at the inn where the carriage stopped and asked my way to the street where my friend was staying. Number sixteen was one of those fine old houses, built a very long time ago, that one still finds in these south German towns. I climbed up four lots of stairs until the only other stairs were those that led up to the roof. There was just one door with a card pinned to it. It was dark there, but I could read the name: Victor Frankenstein.

I moved my hand down the side of the door until I found the bell, and pulled. A long way inside I heard it ring. As I stood there listening to the sound of footsteps coming nearer and nearer I wondered what changes two years had made in my friend. Two years is a long time in the life of a young man.

The footsteps reached the door, and I heard the sound of several locks being turned — it seemed as if he kept

his door very carefully closed. At last it opened, and there he stood — Frankenstein! Yes, it was him, but not the Frankenstein I remembered. Deathly pale, with wild eyes and an uncared-for beard, he was not the young man who had lived the healthy, out-of-door life with me in the mountains of our own country. This thin body on which the clothes hung as if they had been made for someone bigger could not have walked five kilometres. I wondered if he ever left his room.

However, I found no cause for displeasure in the way he received me. After a moment of surprise he came forward and took my hand. A look of joy appeared on his face.

'Henri,' he cried, 'you come at just the right time.'

He drew me inside, then closed the door. This took some time since there were, as I had thought, several large locks. Visitors were clearly neither expected nor wished for.

Frankenstein led the way down a long, dark passage to a book-filled room. A bed stood on one side, looking as if nothing had been done to it for days; and on a table near the window were the remains of several meals. There was dust everywhere, and the last of the evening sun shone with difficulty through the dirty windows. There was a rather unpleasant smell.

After I had given him news about his family and told him the reason for my coming to Ingolstadt, Frankenstein got up and walked about the room excitedly. He did not seem to be thinking at all about what I had just told him.

'Henri,' he said at last. 'You have come just at the very moment when I need your help. The great work which I have been doing for the last year is coming to an end, and I shall soon know whether I have been wasting my time or whether I have pushed scientific

discovery to new heights.' His eyes burned with a strange light. They were like the eyes of a madman.

'My preparations are nearly complete. All I need now are the right conditions for the great experiment to take place.

'Come,' he said, and led the way to a door in a corner of his living room. 'You will see what no other man has seen.'

He threw open the door, and at once the strange smell which I had noticed before became stronger. It was like the smell of bad meat. I could hardly bear it, but my friend seemed not to notice it, and led the way in.

The room was dark, and at first I could only see a mass of wires, glass bottles and jars, and copper and glass pipes. Here and there the blue light of burners made holes in the darkness. And from those places the sound of boiling liquids could be heard.

As my eyes began to see better in the half-darkness I saw that this stuff was arranged round some kind of bath in the middle of the room with a wooden work-table that went all the way round it. Frankenstein was watching me. There was still this strange excitement in his eyes.

'Go on,' he said, 'look inside. See what I have made.'

I bent over the table and looked into the bath. It was filled with a clear liquid. I tried to see deeper into this liquid, but at first all I could see was what looked like hair—fine hair. I bent lower, and as Frankenstein moved a lamp nearer I drew in my breath sharply. It *was* hair— spread out in a golden ring around a face, a head. More. Yes, there was a body in the bath—the body of a man!

Chapter Five

Back in the living room I sat down at the table with the wildest thoughts racing through my mind. As Frankenstein

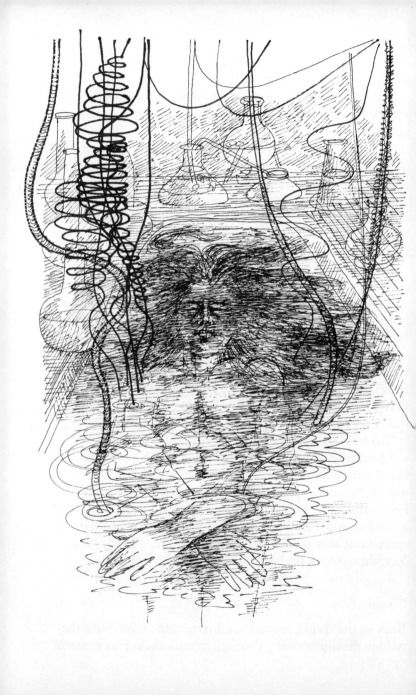

sat down opposite me he looked in the lamplight even
thinner and paler than before. His eyes still shone in an
unnatural way, and his hands would not keep still. Was
he mad? Was the man in the bath someone he had
killed? For the first time in my life, I think, I feared him.

Then he began to speak—in sudden flows of words
which stopped, and then started again. I began to
understand two things: first, that he had hardly spoken
to anyone for months; and secondly, that there was only
one subject which he was able to think about.

He spoke at first of his studies at the university, of his
early experiments, and how little by little he found
himself spending more time in his own rooms than in
listening to his teachers. But it was clear that he could
hardly wait to pass on to the one subject that filled his
mind.

'. . . and so, the science of living bodies became my
chief study — the science of life, and the science of death.
It seemed wrong to me that we knew so much about all
those activities of the human body that make up life;
and yet we did not know how those activities can be set
in movement. To me a human body is like a clock.
Sometimes a clock stops; the spring has not run down,
and all the little wheels are there. But it stops. What do
we do? We pick it up and shake it, and nearly always it
starts again. So I asked myself two questions: first, how
does one make a human body, and secondly, how does
one "shake" it into life?'

'You mean, create life?' I said.

'Yes, create life.' Frankenstein looked at me with a
kind of smile. 'That is an idea which does not please you,
I see.'

'No, it does not please me,' I replied. 'It is not for man
to create life. There are things which man should not
try to know or do. Man has his proper place in nature,

and it is better that he should not try to move out of it,'
I said.

'My dear Henri,' Frankenstein replied, 'if man had
always believed that, there would today be no science,
no learning. Have you never thought of the great
difference between what man could be and what he is?
Have you never looked at man in the streets and then
looked at man in the paintings of the great artists? If you
had the power to create, would you not want to create
the perfect man?'

'If?' I cried, thinking of the body in the bath. 'You
know quite well that you have already created a body.
Do you think you have the power to give it life?'

Frankenstein did not answer. He got up and walked to
the window and opened it. It had been a hot day, and
there was no air in the room. In the distance could be
heard the sound of thunder.

'This is our season of storms,' he said, and looked out
of the window for some minutes. Then he turned and
went on speaking: 'The man of science has no more
power than any other man. Any power more than his
own must be taken from nature. In the next few days
you will see what nature and I can do.' He looked hard
at me. 'You could even help me.'

Help him? Was he asking me to help him create life?
Although I felt horror at his suggestion I also knew that
my friend was offering me part of the honour which
success could bring. But would the experiment succeed?
And — more important — did I really want it to succeed?
As I watched Frankenstein's shaking hand and the
sudden, strange movements of his face, I wondered again
if he was just a little mad. I felt a wish to leave Ingolstadt at
once, until I remembered that I had been sent there by
his father to look after him. It was my duty to stay.

In the days that followed, the more I thought about

the experiment the more it seemed a kind of madness. Could I really join Frankenstein in an act that was against Nature, God and man?

I could, and did. My reasons for doing so were quite simple. This mad plan of his could not possibly succeed. And when it failed, as it certainly would fail, it would be my duty to look after my friend, and help him in his sorrow.

I moved into Frankenstein's rooms, and the first thing I did was to create order and cleanliness, and to make sure that he ate meals at the proper times. Next, I did my best to understand the nature of his discoveries. This was hard, since I was not, like him, a man of science; and if I had been, it might still have been difficult. Even I could see that he had gone far beyond what was known to science at that time. He tried to tell me, but I never did understand, and I ended up simply doing what he told me to do.

It was not, in fact, understanding that I needed most in my work for Frankenstein, but strength of mind. I had to work in a room filled with jars containing every part of the human body: arms, legs, hearts, everything. This was quite disgusting to me, but Frankenstein seemed quite untroubled by it, and picked up these human parts as coolly as a woman in the kitchen picks up a piece of meat.

'In order to get what I need for my work,' he said, 'I have had to go to the hospital, the prison, and even the place where dead bodies are put in the ground. To create life I have had to live side by side with death.'

But it was not the eye-balls which stared at me from inside a jar as I entered the room; or the brain lying in its clear liquid like some strange sea-creature; or the carefully cut off hands waiting for something to get hold of that really troubled me. It was the centre of it

all — the long, white bath where 'he' lay.

I often used to think as we worked that 'he' was asleep, and that we and our doings were part of his dream. Or was it that I was asleep, and that he and Frankenstein and that room were part of mine? At first it was all so strange. But as the days passed I began to lose my fear of him. After all, this was to be the perfect man, and Frankenstein had chosen his parts well. Certainly he had strength and beauty. More than two metres tall, and with that long, golden hair, he appeared more than human. Of the brain that slept behind those closed eyes I knew nothing, but Frankenstein was quite sure that its powers would be no less than the strength of his body.

I had only one doubt.

'So,' I said one day, while we were sitting eating in the living room, 'strength, beauty and cleverness will be his. But what about goodness? Does that perfection which you plan for him go so far?'

'It is all prepared,' said Frankenstein in reply. 'I have plans to take him to live in a place far from the spoiling example of man, where training will bring out his natural goodness. Man is always born good. Evil can only come from man's bad treatment of man. Treat him justly and he will be good.'

I could not answer this. It was what I, too, believed, and for the first time my mind began to enter the world of Frankenstein's hopes and dreams. Suppose, after all, that the dream came true. The body was complete. Could the life-force be made to enter into it?

As if he knew my unspoken thoughts, Frankenstein then spoke: 'I am now ready. I am only waiting for the right conditions.' He went across to the window and opened it. Again I heard the sound of thunder.

'We shall not have long to wait,' he said.

Chapter Six

The next day was hot and the air was heavy. A storm was on the way. Dark clouds gathered in the sky, and by late afternoon it had started to rain in big drops.

All that day Frankenstein had been excited. He seemed to want the storm to come. It was as if he had a place for it in his plans; and as the rain fell faster and faster and the thunder grew louder and louder, he became more and more excited, walking restlessly up and down in front of the open window.

About seven o'clock he suddenly seemed to decide about something. He shut the window and marched into the work-room. I had by this time caught his excitement myself. It was clear that the experiment was about to begin. But when he reappeared a few minutes later my surprise was so great that I started to laugh. He was carrying a child's kite.

'Are we going to play games, then, Victor?' I asked at last.

But my friend remained quite serious and said nothing. Instead of the excitement of a few minutes ago his face now wore the fixed look of someone who knew exactly what he had to do.

I followed him along the passage to the front door, and up the stairs that led to the roof—or rather, to a flat but narrow part of it that lay between two high, pointed parts. On the right I could see a lighted window set in the roof just below its highest point. That must be the window of Frankenstein's work-room.

It was dark and wet, and the wind was very strong. I held the kite while Frankenstein climbed up to the window, which, I noticed, was a little open. I saw him pass his hand through the opening, and in less than a minute he was standing by my side again with the end

of a piece of wire in his hand. I then noticed that there
was also a roll of thin wire tied to the kite. He joined the
kite wire to the wire which came through the window,
and then took the kite from me.

I was glad of this, because the wind was pulling at it
all the time, and I was afraid that it would carry me off
the roof and into the street, five floors below.

But Frankenstein was too deeply interested in what he
was doing to feel fear. Holding the end of the kite in his
teeth he climbed up to the window again, and from
there to the top of the roof. He sat there with one leg on
each side of the roof.

'Up you come, then, Henri,' he called. 'I need you.'

I followed him up, and he put the kite back into my
hands.

'Move along to the other end of the roof and sit facing
the wind. I will hold the wire,' he said.

When we were boys we had loved flying kites; and as
I sat there in the wind and the rain an unexpected feeling
of pleasure ran through me. I lost all my fear of falling.
I could see in the lightning flashes that Frankenstein was
smiling. He felt the same as I did. It was a game now,
and playing it made him feel as if he was a child again.
I think it was the last time I ever saw him as happy as he
was then.

I held the kite up and let the wind take it. Little by
little Frankenstein pulled it up into the stormy night.
Higher and higher it went, and still the wire ran out
through the work-room window. When he thought it
had gone far enough, he tied the wire to something just
inside the window. Then we climbed down from the
roof and returned to the house.

Frankenstein had never forgotten the power of
lightning. The picture of that blackened tree below the
Salève had stuck in both our minds from the time that

we were boys. But while I remembered lightning as a destroyer, Frankenstein had seen further. For him it was a power for creation. Now he was going to try out that power.

At any moment the kite would sail into the very heart of the thundercloud, and a huge electric force would flow down the wire into the work-room. To give life? I still could not believe it.

As we sat silent in the living room listening to the thunder coming nearer and nearer I thought of the perfect man lying in his bath in the next room. Sleeping? Dead? Unborn? I did not know how to think of him. But I saw the lightning flashes and I forget him then. I was too afraid of the lightning. Did Frankenstein know what he was doing in drawing down lightning on the house in this way? He could not know the force with which the lightning would strike. He had an arrangement for leading the electricity to earth, but would it work? It was like sitting next to a bomb of uncertain size, waiting for it to explode.

When it came, of course, I was unprepared. There was a huge noise, a flash, and everything went dark.

It seemed like an age, but it can only have been a minute later when I woke up. I could not hear because of the explosion; nor could I see. I thought at first I had been blinded by the flash, but I soon understood that our lamps had been blown out. I could also smell burning. Frankenstein's earth arrangement had not worked too well, and a great part of the force of the lightning had hit the work-room.

Frankenstein was already on his feet and making his way to the room. The door had been blown open by the explosion and was only just hanging from the door post. Inside was darkness and an even stronger smell of burning. As we entered we felt broken glass under our

feet — and other things that were unpleasantly soft.

The surprise of the lightning had made me forget everything, and it was only when my hands touched the table in the centre of the room that I remembered the experiment. But Frankenstein had not forgotten. He was already bending over the bath, feeling inside with his hands. A distant flash of lightning lit up the room just long enough for me to see a blackened table, a broken bath and the body lying face downwards in a few centimetres of liquid. It was quite still.

'The experiment has failed,' said Frankenstein, and led the way out of the room.

It was the end of all his hopes, and I felt deeply sorry for him. Yet, though I could not say so then, it seemed that things had happened in the best possible way. I had never really wanted it to succeed.

By then, very tired, we threw ourselves down on our beds without even taking the trouble to undress. Before the storm had passed we were deeply asleep.

Chapter Seven

Even though we were tired, too much had happened that night for us to sleep with easy minds. I had dreams — dreams of strange things coming to life on the work-room floor. I dreamed of Elizabeth walking through the streets of Ingolstadt. Pleased and surprised to see her there I walked up to her and kissed her. But as I took my lips away I saw her lips turn from red to the blue-green colour of death. It started to spread across her face, and I forced myself to wake up.

This must have been about half-past four, because I remember the church clock striking the half-hour soon afterwards. I sat up in bed and drew the back of my hand across my face, which was wet with fear and horror.

I looked round. The curtains were closed, and everything was very dark. There was no more thunder, and the storm had passed. My eyes fell upon the open doorway leading to the work-room. It was dark like everywhere else, but less dark, since a little light came in through the window in the roof. As I sat up in bed thinking of the clearing-up we should have to do when daylight came, a shadow moved into the lighter darkness of the doorway. The shadow became a shape. It filled the doorway and then left it empty again. It had passed into the room where I was. My blood ran cold. Something was standing very close to my bed.

Then I heard a sound from the other bed. Frankenstein was also awake. He suddenly pulled the curtains open, and the unkind, grey light of early morning flowed into the room to show — what can I say? I could see at once that it was the body in the bath, now alive and breathing. But where was perfection? Where was the man-god of Frankenstein's dreams? Was this the end of the great experiment?

There he stood, unclothed, wet and shining, his long hair hanging down over his chest. If he had stood up straight he would have been a giant — as it was, he was nearly two metres tall — but his back was bent, and his arms hung in front of him like those of a huge monkey. As for his face, the beauty of the body in the bath had gone with the lightning. Instead of the rosy white of the skin before life, the living skin was yellow and dry like old paper, and was stretched across the bones like a piece of clothing that was too small. This left the teeth uncovered, so that he wore an unnatural smile all the time. Lightning burns and lines where the pieces of skin had been joined together marked the rest of his body; and the whites of his narrow eyes were the colour of blood. He was a monster!

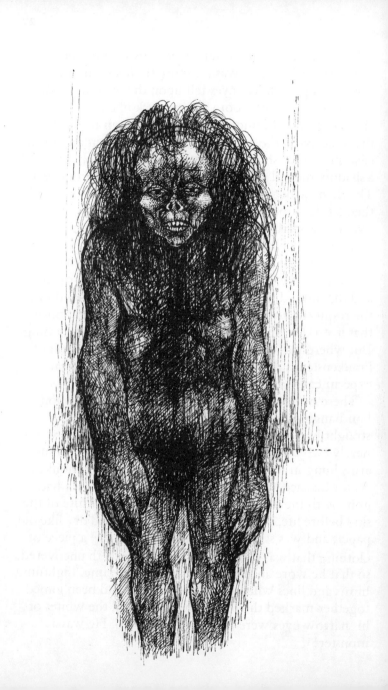

No one spoke. The only sound was that of the liquid dropping off the ends of the Monster's hair on to the floor. Frankenstein was filled with horror. He stared at the Monster and the Monster stared back at him. As for me, after the first surprise I felt nothing but plain, simple fear. But as the minutes passed I began to understand that there was no reason for fear. This was not a wild animal. If he had meant to attack us he would already have done so by now. He was no more certain what to do than we were. As he stared in that fixed way at Frankenstein, it almost seemed as if he knew that he was looking at his maker. He even began to look friendly. Did he want to thank the man who had given him life?

Almost as this thought passed through my mind he took a step forward, went down on his knees and stretched out a hand. I think he was going to kiss Frankenstein's foot. But whatever he meant to do, he did not have a chance to do it, because, with a cry of horror, Frankenstein kicked out, and the Monster fell back. He got up very quickly, which showed that although he looked heavy he was strong and active. Now it was his turn to look surprised, and Frankenstein, seeing that the Monster was not as dangerous as he had thought, took his chance. He picked up a heavy stick and stepped forward.

'Out!' he cried. 'Out of my rooms! Out of my sight! You are disgusting!'

Still with a look of hurt surprise on his face, and without saying a word, the Monster turned, and Frankenstein ran after him down the passage, where the front door, pulled in by the force of the explosion, lay wide open. He ran out and disappeared down the stairs.

I went straight to the window and looked out. After a minute the Monster came into the street. He seemed uncertain what to do, but in the end he ran off through

the still empty town towards the main gate.

'He is disgusting,' said Frankenstein. 'I cannot bear to think of him.'

'But he is yours. You made him,' I said.

'He was a mistake.'

'Perhaps, but he was *your* mistake. He is yours, and he knows it. Did you not see how he treated you as his master? And what did you do? You drove him away. That was neither good nor wise.'

Frankenstein grew pale at my words. His whole body shook. 'He is *not* mine. He was a mistake, I tell you — an experiment that went wrong. He is not even human. I owe him nothing!'

'But, my dear fellow, what is going to happen?' I asked. 'You cannot just let him run off like that.'

'Nature has made a mistake, and, as Nature always does, she will put her mistake right in her own way. This creature cannot live. You could see it was incomplete. It will die a natural death and there will be no more difficulties.'

This did not seem a right and proper answer. I tried again: 'But do you not feel you have some duty——'

'Duty!' cried Frankenstein in an excited voice. 'Do not speak to me of duty. I have spent too long in this town wasting my life in useless study. I shall return to Geneva. I shall go back home. Yes, I shall leave today!'

Chapter Eight

In this sudden way my friend's stay in Ingolstadt came to an end. He quickly filled a bag with necessary things for his journey and asked me to send the rest of his things on to Geneva later. He could not wait to leave, and was most happy to find a place on the eight o'clock carriage to Ulm.

As I stood there in the market-place waving goodbye, I began to think about the difficulties, and even dangers, that Frankenstein was leaving me to face. What reason could I give for his sudden disappearance? Far worse to deal with was the equally sudden appearance of an unclothed monster in the streets of the town.

When caught, the Monster would surely lead the townspeople back to Frankenstein's rooms. The authorities would ask questions, and I had no idea how I would answer them.

I returned to the house and spent the rest of the morning there, waiting for a loud ring at the door. But it did not come. Nor did it come that afternoon or the next day. What had happened? Had the Monster found a hiding-place in the town. This was not easy to find in a small place like Ingolstadt. Or had Frankenstein been right about Nature and her mistakes? Had the Monster in some strange way just disappeared into the air?

The next day I decided to find out in the way that everybody found things out in Ingolstadt. I went down to the market-place.

'What news?' I asked, as I bought some eggs from an old woman in a corner of the square.

'The price of eggs is up,' she replied.

I decided to take a chance, and went on: 'I heard some talk of a strange visitor to the town.'

'Hah!' she said. 'Yesterday's news. And if you ask me, I'd say he'd been drinking.'

'Who?'

'Why, the gate-keeper — that Kaspar. He shouldn't be on the gate. I don't mind who he lets out of the town, but one day he'll let the French army in.'

'I heard something of this story,' I lied. 'What exactly did Kaspar say he saw?'

'Well, it was early on Monday morning — I'm only

telling you what he said — and he'd just opened the gates and gone back into the gate-house when some kind of wild man without any clothes on ran by. He went out to try and catch him, but he was already too far away.'

I laughed. 'So that was it. Another fairy story.'

As I walked back to the house I felt as if a great weight had been lifted from me. What luck! The Monster had escaped from the town, and the one person who had seen him was not believed. No doubt Frankenstein was right. He would make his way into the forest and die, and no one would ever know anything about it.

The rest of the summer passed happily as I worked hard at my studies. I had to, since I had already lost too much time in helping Frankenstein. My studies went well, and when the university year began in September I was properly prepared. I had heard nothing from Frankenstein, and had almost stopped thinking about the whole unhappy business of the Monster.

However, one Saturday morning towards the end of the month I was again buying food in the market, when I found myself talking to an old wood-cutter who lived in the forest about ten kilometres to the south of the town. He said that there had been stories of strange things going on in the forest. . .a child frightened at a spring. . .a face at a window. . .food and clothing stolen. He had seen nothing himself, but he had met those who had. There was talk of a 'wild man'.

'The farmers living on the edge of the forest won't let their children go into it any more,' the old man said. 'But we who live in the forest — we have to work, wild men or no wild men.'

I laughed and tried not to show too much interest. But the very next day I put on my walking shoes, took my

stick in my hand and left the town early in the morning. I made my way along the main road to the south and turned off into that part of the forest where the wood-cutter said the wild man had been seen.

I spent all that day talking to those few people who really lived in the forest itself, wood-cutters and bird-catchers. It soon became clear from what they told me that there was indeed a wild man in the woods, even though nobody I spoke to had been very close to him. He had done no harm. He had not tried to attack anybody. When seen he had always tried to run away. Nobody had dared to follow him; and even if they had, it seemed that he could run so fast that it would be difficult to catch him.

One thing was certain: the Monster had not died.

I returned to Ingolstadt knowing that I had to find the Monster and talk to him. Why I wanted to do this I am not quite sure, unless it was the feeling that those who had made him owed him something. But there may also have been another reason. Although seemingly harmless now, the Monster might not remain so. It was somebody's duty to make friends with him and make sure that he did not turn against the human race.

I spent the next four Sundays looking for him. The forest was huge, and I knew it would be no use wandering along its many paths hoping to meet him by chance. Better to wait for him to come to me. So, knowing that he had to eat and drink I used to hide where the wild fruits of the forest grew, and by springs unvisited by men. These were the places where he would go. Even so, for a long time I had no success.

Then one day at the beginning of October, before all the leaves had fallen, I was lying down reading a book behind a bush near a spring, when I heard the sound of

feet on dry leaves. I looked up to see the leaves of a bush about fifteen metres in front of me being pushed aside by two huge, brown hands. Then a face appeared. My blood ran cold. He was far more frightful than I remembered. Did I really dare to speak to this creature?

The leaves moved back, and a little later the 'wild man' appeared in front of the spring.

Though still the same monster that I had last seen running through the streets of Ingolstadt, he had changed. He wore no shoes, but he had found other clothing; and his look and manner were not quite those of a wild man. The strangest thing about him was that he carried a basket full of wild fruits. Where did this basket come from, and why did he not eat the fruit straight off the bushes?

He stood there for a minute, his nose spread wide as he smelt the wind. Luckily it was against me.

Hardly daring to breathe, I watched him fall to his knees and drink like an animal from the spring. Then he stood up, picked up his basket and went off the way he had come with a strange half walking, half running action.

I had meant to speak to him there at the spring, but the sight of that basket made me think again. Where was he taking it to? In what cave or rough hut did he live. My curiosity being awakened I decided to follow him as well as I could. And so, after letting him get some way in front, I came out from behind my bush and went after him.

Chapter Nine

He was not easy to follow. At times he moved so fast that I could not keep at all near him. At other times, while looking for fruit, he moved along very slowly. Sometimes I came up very close to him indeed, so that

I was in danger of being seen. In the end I lost him completely.

This was bad. It was not just that I had lost him. I had been following him for about half an hour, and it was late afternoon. I was in a part of the forest where I had never been before, and was now quite lost. It was too cold to spend a night out at this time of the year, and I would be lucky to find a house.

However, luck had not quite left me that day. A surprise was waiting for me. Going on towards a lighter part of the forest in front of me, I came to an open space among the trees, in the middle of which stood a little wooden house. The smoke of a fire rose straight up in the still, October air. At least, I thought, there must be somebody there who could tell me where I was.

But just as I was about to walk across to the house, I heard the sound of someone moving through the forest on the other side. I stopped where I was, and a few minutes later I saw the Monster making his way round the house. Still with his basket he entered the little garden, pushed open the front door and disappeared inside.

I knelt down behind some bushes and looked at the house. It was well kept, with a vegetable garden in front surrounded by a simple fence. Nicely cut firewood stood carefully placed against the side of the house.

'This is not the house of a monster,' I said to myself. 'Who does it belong to, and what is he doing here?'

After about ten minutes the door opened and the Monster appeared again, but not alone. This time an old man was with him, and a young girl — a very pretty young girl. I was too far away to hear what they were saying, but they were certainly all talking — proof that the Monster could talk. After a few minutes he went off with that half run of his into the forest again.

I waited for the old man and the girl to go back into

the house, then I walked across and rang at the front
door. It opened, and the girl stood in front of me.

'Good day,' I said. 'I am a poor student of Ingolstadt
and have lost my way walking in the forest. Could you
please tell me where I am?'

She smiled uncertainly, but said nothing.

I went on: 'If it is not too much trouble I should also
like a drink of water.' She made no answer, and I began
to wonder. Was she so much of a country girl that she
did not understand my way of talking? She did not look
a country girl at all.

'Who is it, Agatha?' called the old man from inside.
This time I was really surprised. He had spoken in
French.

'It is a student from Ingolstadt,' she replied. 'I think
he wants something to drink.'

'Bring him in, then. We have too few visitors here.
Offer him whatever we have.'

I followed her into the cottage, where I found the old
man sitting by the fire, and a young man writing at a
table with books all round him. The shelves round the
room were also filled with books — mostly in French,
I noticed. This was not a family of simple forest workers.

I very soon learned their whole story. Their name was
de Lacy, and they were indeed French — from Paris. As
a result of unjust laws they had had to leave France.
With the small amount of money they had been able to
take with them they had settled in this quiet place, living
the simple life and enjoying the pleasures of nature and
study. Old de Lacy was blind, and Agatha and her
brother Felix spent most of the evenings reading aloud
to him.

For a time we sat and talked pleasantly of Paris and
Geneva. But I had not forgotten the real reason for my
visit, and I began to turn the subject of our talk towards

the Monster.

'Do you never feel too much alone here?' I asked. 'It must be hard to live without friends or neighbours.'

'Indeed, we have little company,' replied the old man. 'A passing wood-cutter may sometimes call, but we have had no visitor here for weeks.'

I did not know what to say to that. I had seen the Monster come and go with my own eyes. Was the old man lying? If so, I must not make him appear to be lying. 'Perhaps it is not every passer-by who calls in,' I said. 'I thought I heard someone in the woods on the other side of your house just before I came to your door.'

Agatha smiled. 'That was no passer-by,' she said. 'He lives in a little hut behind the house. He is a very strange person, and very ugly to look at, but there is some goodness in him. He cuts wood for us and gathers wild fruits in the forest. I believe the other people in the forest call him "the wild man", but he is quite safe to be with.'

'He may be wild,' added Felix, 'but I think he is quite clever. He has learned to speak French only by listening to us. He also listens when we read to Father. He knows more than we think.'

'But where does he come from?' I asked. 'Has he ever told you where he used to live before?'

'We once asked him,' said Felix, 'but the question seemed to cause him such unhappiness that we never asked him again. He seems to have no family, and no friends except for us. I think that when he was young his family was so disgusted by his ugliness that they left him in the forest to die. I have heard of children like this being kept alive by animals, and I think this is possibly what happened to him.'

'I should like to meet him some time,' I said. 'Your

story interests me because I think he may be an old servant of my friend. He disappeared some time ago, and I would like to be able to tell my friend that he is well. When he comes back, tell him that his master, Frankenstein, sends him his best wishes. He would like to help him, but he does not know where his servant has gone. Now he has gone back home to Geneva.'

If I had only known the results of my well-meaning words I would never have breathed the name of Frankenstein in that house. But what Felix had said about parents leaving their children to die in the forest made me think again about Frankenstein's treatment of the Monster. I still hoped to get him to do his duty.

'We shall be pleased to see you here any time,' said the old man. 'But it is already dark. Can we offer you a bed for the night?'

Although nothing would have pleased me more than to stay longer with this pleasant family, I had to be at the university the next morning. So Felix, who knew the forest well, even in the dark, offered to guide me as far as a wide path which would take me back to the road.

I was back at Ingolstadt just before the gate closed.

Chapter Ten

Next Sunday there was something happening at the university. We all had to go to church, and I could not escape from it. The Sunday after that it rained so heavily that it would have been madness to go out that day. I would have been wet through, even before I had gone from the house to the town gate. So it was three weeks before I was able to return to the forest.

By that time the leaves had all turned brown and were falling fast. It had been so different when I followed the

Monster through a still green forest. I could not have done it now without being seen or heard by him. It was also true that he could not follow me without my knowing it. From time to time I stopped and listened for the sound of feet on the dry leaves that lay thick in the paths. But there was never anything to be heard, and I felt sure that I was quite alone.

My thoughts soon turned from the Monster to Agatha. It seemed all wrong that a pretty young girl like her should waste her life in that dark forest with no one to see her. I would like to know her better. I decided to ask her and her brother to visit me at Ingolstadt one day.

It was with these pleasant thoughts in my mind that I followed the path to the open space where the de Lacys' cottage stood. There I stopped as if awakened from a dream.

My first thought was that I had come the wrong way: that I had arrived by mistake at a different place in the forest. I looked and looked again with growing horror, but saw that I had made no mistake. This was the place, but the cottage had gone. Where it once stood were a few low stone walls and a mass of blackened wood. The whole house had been destroyed by fire.

How long I stood staring I do not know. It was like being in a dream — but which was the dream, my visit three weeks before, or my standing there in front of the burnt remains? Nothing seemed real any more, and I found it hard to make myself walk across to the remains of the cottage.

Being mostly built of wood, it must have burnt down very quickly: and if the fire had started at night when the de Lacys were asleep they must surely have died. As for the Monster, had he died with the de Lacys or escaped with them? The hut at the back, where he had lived,

remained unburnt, but it also showed no marks of being lived in. Were they all alive or dead?

I kept turning this question over in my mind, not wishing to face the one sure way of finding the answer — by digging in the remains of the house. But in the end I knew that this was what I had to do. The roof had fallen in and covered everything, so I went across to the vegetable garden to find something to dig with. Then, praying that I would not find what I feared to find, I began to dig.

After trying two or three places and finding nothing worse than a few half-burnt books and some broken plates, I began to feel better. Perhaps they had escaped after all. Then I tried again at the back of the house. I started by pulling away a bit of the roof with my hands. And there underneath — even after fifty years the horror of it is as real to me as it ever was — a dried-up human arm reached out through the mass of burnt remains. A ring hung from one of the bony fingers. I had seen that ring before. The hand that had opened the cottage door to me three weeks before had worn it. It was the hand of Agatha!

With a long cry of pain I ran into the forest not knowing or caring where I went, trying only to lose myself and my thoughts among the trees. It was as I had feared. The whole family must have died in the fire. And the Monster? Had he, too, died with the family that had made him their friend? So many frightful possibilities ran through my mind. I did not want to think of any of them, but went on running along the forest paths until, tired and breathless, I reached the road to Ingolstadt.

The next day I wrote to Frankenstein telling him all that had happened. 'I can only suppose,' I wrote, 'that the Monster has died in the fire. If you feel that you did

wrong in making him, and that I did wrong in seeking him out in the forest, his death undoes all our mistakes.'

He did not reply, but I did not think this was unusual. I knew that he must still have family business to deal with after being away from home for so long. Besides, he never wrote any letters unless he really had something to say. However, it was a little surprising that Elizabeth did not write, as she had written me several letters before.

I tried to forget, through hard work, what had happened in the forest. And if I was not successful in this, at least my studies began to go well — so well that I wanted them to go even better, and I planned to stay at Ingolstadt and work all through the holidays. However, at the beginning of December I received a letter from my father with the most strange and frightful news. William, my friend's little brother, had been murdered!

This, in itself, was hard to believe, but when my father went on to say that he had been murdered by Justine Moritz, the very person whose job it was to look after him, I began to think he was going mad. However, a cutting from a Geneva newspaper sent with the letter told the same story. From this and what my father told me I tried to put the story together.

One afternoon early in November, Justine and the child had gone for a walk near the Frankensteins' country house at Belrive. William was wearing a heavy gold chain round his neck with a little picture of his mother hanging from it. It was not a good thing for a young child to wear when going out for a walk, but he had asked so much that in the end Elizabeth let him wear it just for that afternoon, since he promised to be careful with it.

It was this chain, it seemed, which had caused his death. Justine had taken him into some woods and put her

hands round his neck until he was dead. She then ran off with the gold chain. She reached Thonon before she was caught.

'We all hope she will be punished by the city as she will surely be punished by God,' said my father at the end of his letter.

I sat back in my chair not knowing what to think. I read the letter and the cutting again and again to make sure I had not made any mistake. It was plain enough, but I still could not believe it. I knew Justine. She was a kind and loving girl. There was no one she loved more than little William—unless, perhaps, it was Victor.

No, I thought. There must be some mistake; and although the judges must already have passed judgement on the poor girl I decided to return to Geneva at once to see if there was anything I could do, either for her or for the Frankensteins.

Chapter Eleven

I arrived in Geneva a few days later at about nine o'clock in the morning. Knowing that the gate would be shut before I could reach the city, I had spent the night before at the nearby town of Nyon. I then took a boat along the north shore of the lake to Geneva.

The place where the ships tied up did not seem very active for the time of the day, but this did not, by itself, surprise me. However, when I passed through the city gates I could no longer fail to notice the emptiness of the streets. It was clear, bright weather for the time of the year, and the hard-working people of the city should all have been at their businesses. But everywhere I looked, shops and offices were closed. Only a little thought was enough to tell me that I had made no mistake about the date. It was not a Sunday or a public holiday.

Soon I noticed another thing. The few people who were in the streets were all going the same way — towards the opposite side of the city; and they were in a hurry. They could only be going to Plainpalais, a piece of flat, open land on the far side of the River Arve where the men of the city, doing their soldier training, used to march up and down on Sunday mornings. It was also — as I remembered with sudden fear — the place of public hangings!

I started to run: across the old market-place, up the street where the city government meets, until, breathless, I joined a large, silent crowd on the city walls. I could see nothing, so I pulled myself up into the window of a house. Below the walls I could see an even larger crowd. All Geneva was there — and more, since there were many people from the small towns and villages around.

In the middle of the crowd was a raised wooden floor with a post in the middle and a rope hanging from the post. Among the few people standing there was a girl in a black dress. Even at that distance I knew it was Justine.

This crowd was not like any other crowd I had ever known. It was somehow strange and frightening that, although so large, it made so little noise. The air was thick with hate. They wanted that poor, frightened girl in black to die; and it was nearly time for her to do so.

As the last prayer was said, and the rope was placed around her neck I jumped down from my place in the window. My eyes filled with tears and I could watch no more. I turned away from the crowd into the peace and quiet of the Rue des Granges. But I had not gone far before I heard a deep cry of pleasure rise from the crowd, and I knew that Justine was no more. I stopped and placed my hand on the wall of a nearby house. Suddenly I felt quite ill.

As I stood there in the empty street trying to gather

my thoughts, it came to my mind that the house I was resting against was well known to me. It was the town house of the Frankensteins. I walked on to the front door, which I found a little open. I pushed my way in. There was no servant in the hall, so I called. All was quiet. Had everybody gone to the hanging?

As a close friend of the family I felt free to walk upstairs; and finding the door of my friend's room open, I went in.

At first I thought the room was empty like the rest of the house, but then I saw somebody kneeling in a corner, his face pressed against the wall, and as still and silent as if he was dead.

'Victor!' I called quietly. He made no reply. I began to think he really was dead. I got hold of him and pulled him out of his corner. His face was wet with tears. 'Victor, it's me, Henri. I have come back from Ingolstadt to help you.' He still made neither sound nor movement.

'To help you,' I said again.

'I am beyond help,' he said at last.

'None of us are beyond help...except (I could not help adding)...poor Justine.' As I spoke her name Frankenstein let out an unhappy cry.

'I could not help her,' he said. 'I tried...God knows how hard I tried, but they would not listen. I told them again and again who had killed William, but I had no proof. In the end they thought I was mad.'

'Then it was not Justine who killed him?'

'How could you ever have thought it was? That sweet young girl...' His voice broke. 'You knew her. It is enough.'

'Then who did kill him?' I asked.

'Do you need to ask? Why, it was *him*.'

'Him?'

'Yes, yes, the one I made and gave life to, who has followed me here to destroy my happiness.'

The Monster had followed him here? Had he not died in the fire, then, together with the de Lacys? I began to understand the full horror of what had happened. I had told the de Lacys where Frankenstein lived so that they might tell the Monster. It was my turn now to feel as Frankenstein felt. Was it really because of me that two people who never did anybody any harm had died. To think that I had once felt sorry for this creature. Why, why did I have to search for him in the forest? The thought that I was the cause of so much unhappiness was almost too much to bear.

I had told Frankenstein in my letter about my first visit to the de Lacys. Now I told him again about the fire and their frightful end. That, at least, owed nothing to me. Then I told him how my words to the de Lacys had led the Monster to Geneva.

My friend listened in silence. But it was clear even before he began to speak that he did not think I was the cause of these evils.

'He is devilishly clever,' he said. 'He would have found his way to us without your help — be sure of that. I know you meant well; but he does not return good for the good actions he receives. I have made something unchangeably evil, and I have not yet learned the full cost of his making.'

'Surely,' I replied, 'all creatures are born with the possibility of becoming good or evil. This monster may yet be changed. Did not the de Lacys' kindness bring out the good in him?'

'Yes, and how did he return their kindness? Do you think that they died by chance? No, they were destroyed by him just as surely as my William was.'

I stared at him in horror at the idea. Did he mean that

this creature had set light to the house of a family that had made him their friend? I could not believe it. There was no proof. And yet Frankenstein had planted doubt in my mind. If he really had killed William, there was nothing, however evil, that he could not have done. But again — did he murder William? I asked Frankenstein to tell me his story.

'You know,' he said, 'why I returned to Geneva in August after the failure of my experiment. It was not because I feared the monster that I had made, or the people of Ingolstadt. I simply felt that I had to escape from a town where I had wasted so much of my life. I knew that it was time to go home.

'For some months I lived happily with my family and began to make plans for further studies. I decided to leave science, and was thinking of studying music. Then one day, quite without warning, my happiness was destroyed for ever.

'Justine and William went out every day when the weather was fine. There was nothing to make us think that this day would be any different from all the other days: nothing in Justine's manner to suggest that she was planning murder. There are two stories about what happened after they left the house, Justine's and the court's. You have, I am sure, heard the court's. Your father must have written to tell you all about it. Now let me tell you Justine's.

'This is how she told it: after leaving home they walked up the hill, as they often did, to a little wood about half a kilometre away. Just before they got to the wood Justine sat down on a rock to do some needlework, while William picked flowers. He must have gone into the wood, because a little later she heard his voice coming from the trees together with another deeper, rougher voice. As she stood up to see who he was with,

she heard him give a cry of fear. She ran into the wood and was just in time to see him being carried off under the arm of a huge, ugly, hairy man with no clothes on.

'She tried to pull William away from him, and succeeded for a short time in weakening his hold on the boy. But this only made the man seize William by the neck with one hand, and hold him at arm's length away from Justine. After keeping her off for a time with the other hand, he at last struck her so suddenly and so hard that she fell to the ground.

'When she woke up she found herself in the same place, and William beside her dead, with black finger-marks on his neck. His broken chain lay nearby. The man had quite disappeared.

'Think how the poor girl must have felt. Would they say it was all because she had let William go off into the wood by himself that he had died? Would they believe her story of a wild man whom nobody had ever seen before? All kinds of thoughts must have been mixed up in her mind; and I can understand why she did not want to go back to the house. So, with the gold chain still in her hand, she made the great mistake of running away. As you know, she got as far as Thonon, where her wild looks and strange manner caught the attention of the authorities. They held her there. Then the news of the murder arrived from Geneva.'

'Are you quite sure that the wild man in Justine's story was . . . your monster?' I asked.

'I was able to question Justine closely in prison, and what she told me makes me think that he may have changed since you last saw him. You say that in the forest he wore clothes. He now seems to have given up clothes completely, and there has been a growth of hair all over his body. But I have no doubt it is the same creature.'

'What did you do when Justine was taken to prison?'

Frankenstein turned pale. 'Everything... everything I could to save her. I would have died in her place in Plainpalais this morning if they had let me. But the trouble was that the authorities would not believe me. When I started talking about a monster I had made, they thought I was mad. And even if they had believed me, I could not have proved that it was the Monster that had killed William.

'I went to the wood, and found marks of feet, but they were not very clear. Besides it rained heavily the next night. So when I showed them to the authorities they said that they meant nothing. In the end I saw that my only hope of saving her was to prove that there really was a monster; and to do this I had to find him. I spent the next three weeks searching the mountains all around, but with no success.'

'And Elizabeth?' I asked. 'How did she take it?'

'Even without knowing what I knew, she did not believe that Justine was a murderer, and she did what she could to save her. But Justine would not save herself. She seemed to think that she was in some way the cause of William's death, and she no longer wished to live. She did not even try to say anything in her own favour in court. In the end even Elizabeth came to doubt her story.'

Frankenstein looked very tired. 'You must rest now,' I said. 'You trouble yourself too much, thinking that they died because of you. They did not.'

'It *was* because of me,' he replied. 'And as for rest, there will be no more rest for me until I find and destroy the creature that I have made.'

Chapter Twelve

I did not go back to Ingolstadt that winter. The needs of

my friends were more important to me than my studies. Besides, Geneva had libraries, and I could just as well keep up my studies there.

It was not too hard a winter, and the snow did not lie long down by the lake. But it was thick enough in the high mountains, where Frankenstein was sure the Monster was hiding; too thick for anyone to search out his hiding-place. However, that was not exactly what Frankenstein planned to do. By following the snow-line he hoped to find the marks of the Monster's feet as he came down from the high ground to feed, and this was how my friend spent the next few months. As winter turned to spring, and the snow fell back, he was able to go higher and higher up the valleys. But never once did he find marks made by any animal bigger than a mountain goat.

Sometimes on a sunny spring day we used to go out together in a boat on the lake, and if Elizabeth was not too busy she joined us. At times like these it felt as if we were children again, and I, at least, was happy.

But did Frankenstein's troubled spirit ever find rest? I used to watch him hanging over the side of the boat looking down into the water so clear that one could see fish swimming about even five metres down. But I knew that his thoughts were not there but high in the mountains. In his mind he was following the marks of huge feet through the snow to the mouth of some smelly cave.

As spring turned into summer Frankenstein began to lose hope of ever finding the Monster. The thought even came into his head that he might not have to kill him. Perhaps he had died of cold in the mountains. Even if he was still alive he seemed to have lost interest in the Frankenstein family.

August came, and old Frankenstein told his son to

take a holiday.

'You need a change, Victor,' he said. 'You cannot sit around the house doing nothing all summer. Take Henri with you up to Chamonix. It will be cool there, and you can walk in the mountains. Perhaps also you will find time to think about your studies. I wish you would return to science.'

It was clear from Victor's face, when he heard this, that he would do nothing to make his father's last wish come true. But he was not against going to Chamonix, the village that lay at the foot of Europe's highest mountain. The very next day we set off together on horseback along the river Arve, which flowed down from the Chamonix valley.

It was an exciting journey. As we went higher, the valley became narrower, and the road became a rocky path. In many places we thought it safer to lead our horses on foot. But as the path grew more dangerous the country around became more wild and beautiful. At times it was almost frightening. Great glaciers flowed down almost to the path. And we often heard the thunderous sound of great masses of snow falling off the nearby mountains. Sometimes the snowy, round top of Mont Blanc showed above the needle-like rocks below it.

All this natural beauty seemed to excite Frankenstein, and I began to wonder whether the holiday would do him the good that his father hoped for.

At last we reached Chamonix near the bottom of the Mer de Glace, the greatest glacier in Europe, a huge river of ice coming down from the heights of Mont Blanc. In these days the village had little to offer the traveller, but we found a room in a farmer's house, and every day we went for walks in the mountains.

On the fifth day of our stay we decided to climb to a point on the edge of the Mer de Glace where it was

possible to look right over the ice. By this time of the
year the snow on the lower part of the glacier had
disappeared, and one could see the long cracks that went
deep down into the ice. It was then possible, if one took
care, to cross the glacier.

As soon as we came in sight of it, Frankenstein knew
that this was just what he had to do. I did not feel as
strong a wish to take this walk as he did. Too many men
going to shoot wild goats had fallen into these icy, green
holes and had never been seen again. However, I knew
that two people were safer on the ice than one, so off we
went together.

It was certainly exciting on the glacier. Using our iron-
pointed sticks which dug into the ice, we carefully
walked round the edges of the cracks. There were so
many of them that it was impossible to walk straight
across the ice; and by the time that we had got to the
thin finger of rock that reached up from the bottom of
the glacier, separating it into two parts, we could see
that it would take a long time to get right across.

We never did get right across. At this point an
enjoyable mountain walk turned into something strange
and frightening.

From the rock where we had sat down to rest we
could see a long way up the glacier. And as we looked,
we both could see that we were not alone. Far above us
a human shape appeared to be moving down the ice
towards us. From the start we were surprised. Few
people ever even crossed the glacier, but fewer still
came down it. As we watched, we noticed something
even stranger. Whoever it was was moving very fast, and
in a straight line towards us.

'But this is unbelievable,' said Frankenstein. 'He must
be jumping across the cracks.'

As he came nearer we could see that was just what he

was doing. He was flying over cracks that must have been seven or eight metres across. What human being could jump so far for so long?

'It's him,' cried Frankenstein. And indeed it was the Monster — so long sought without success, and now coming to meet us at a time when we had nothing more than sticks to hold him off with. As he climbed up the rocks just below us I could see the strength in that hairy body. How easy it would be for him to tear us from the rock and throw us one after the other into the nearest crack in the ice! Without thinking, we had put ourselves completely in his power. This could be the end of us both!

Chapter Thirteen

The Monster came on until he was about ten metres from us, then stopped. He appeared to be staring at us, but his eyes were so hidden by the dirty hair that hung down over his face that it was difficult to know what he was thinking.

We looked at each other for some minutes in silence. Then he moved nearer, bringing with him a strong animal smell. If he had meant to attack us, he would surely have done so by now.

Instead he began to speak. It was the first time we had heard his voice, which was deep and rough. But the manner of his speaking did not prepare us for what he said. We were surprised to find that behind that voice lay a thinking, feeling person.

'You may wonder why I have come to meet you here,' he said, fixing his look upon Frankenstein. 'It is not to destroy you, as you would destroy me if you had the power to do so. It is to tell you my story. When you have heard it, then, perhaps, you will tell me whether

I owe anything to you or to any man.

'First let me tell you how I found myself alone, cold, hungry and unclothed in the forest near Ingolstadt. What my life before had been I did not know, except that I remembered being in a room and you looking with disgust at me and shouting.

'I learned quickly how to live in the forest. There were springs for water and wild fruits for food. My stomach learned to take the roughest and poorest food. After all, I was not quite human, as you well know. At first I was cold, and had to walk about at night to keep warm, sleeping during the day when the sun shone. Later I found clothes hanging outside the houses of villagers. I saw what humans wore, and wished to wear the same, since at that time I still foolishly hoped to be received as one of the human race.'

The Monster's voice at this point shook with feeling. He went on: 'But humans were disgusted by me. One day I decided to enter a village to see what would happen. And what did happen? The children ran away, the women cried out in horror and the men threw stones at me. The body that you gave me disgusted them as it disgusted you. In the end it disgusted me. I decided to go deeper into the forest to die — as you no doubt hoped I would. It was then that I came upon the house of the de Lacys.

'At first I used to watch them from behind the trees. I used to see Felix go off into the forest and return with firewood. I saw the old man sitting in the sun. But when I saw Agatha I put away all thoughts of dying. I thought that she was as much above all the other human beings as I was below them. I wanted to be her friend. I wanted to be a friend to them all. So I began to gather wood in the forest every day and lay it beside their door; and sometimes wild fruits — early in the morning before they

got up.

'One morning, just as I was putting the wood there, the door suddenly opened, and there stood Agatha. When she saw me she was surprised and frightened, but she did not shut the door. She gave me food, and I stayed. They all began asking me questions, but I could not answer them then. However, as I visited the house again and again, I began to understand and speak their language. In the end I moved into the little hut behind the house. And when Agatha and Felix used to read to their father in the evenings, I listened, and learned about the world outside the forest. I even learned to read, myself, and learned from history that human beings hardly treated each other any better than they treated me.

'I learned, too, the meaning of words like brother, sister, father and mother. I saw that I had none of these. I could not even remember having been a child. Had I forgotten all my early life, I used to wonder. Or was there nothing to forget? Could it be that I had not been born, but made already fully grown? If so, who had made me? All I could remember was a face. But whose face was it?

'The answer to my question came by chance. A man called at the cottage one day while I was in the forest and talked to the de Lacys about my "master", Frankenstein, of Geneva. At last I knew my maker's name and where he lived. One day, I decided, I would go and seek him. But before I could do this, something happened which turned me against the human race for ever.

'I saw that in the world people lived in families, but I had no family. I knew that families could be made by two people who loved each other. From the time I first saw her, Agatha had seemed to me like something from

another world; and the longer I lived with the de Lacys the more I grew to love her.

'One day when Felix had gone to the town, and the old father was asleep in his room, I found Agatha reading a book under the apple tree in the garden. I knelt down in front of her and told her of my love. I took her hand and kissed it.

'She pulled it back as if I had laid a red-hot iron there. Without a word she threw down her book and ran into the house. She stayed in her room all that afternoon. She did not have to speak: her face told me everything I needed to know. It had had the same look as the first human face I ever saw — a look of horror, fear, disgust.

'I knew then that I could never find happiness in human company, and ran off into the thickest part of the forest. For days I lay there, turning my sorrows over and over in my mind. Why should these humans treat me as they did? Was I just an animal to work for them? They had used me but never loved me.

'It was then that I decided to destroy them. One night when they were all asleep, I came quietly to their house. First I made sure that nobody could get out, by rolling large rocks against the doors. Next I went to the place built into the outside wall of the house where Agatha used to make bread. I blew the dying fire to life again, and with a handful of dried grass I carried fire to the edge of the roof. The roof was made of dry stuff and burnt easily. I stood aside and waited.' The Monster's voice stopped. He closed his eyes and rubbed his hairy body with his great hands. He smiled as he remembered.

'After a time I heard cries from inside. But the windows were small, the old man was blind, and there was thick smoke. They died; I laughed; and ran off into the forest. I was on my way to Geneva.

'I travelled by night so that I should not meet anybody.

Because I no longer wished to belong to the human race I gave up wearing clothes, and soon found that the cold did not trouble me any more. Coming down from the mountains at the east end of the Lake of Geneva, I swam across the lake to Savoy, and went on towards Geneva along the south shore.

'At that point I knew I was faced with a difficulty. I knew that Geneva was a large town, and I had no way of finding where my maker lived. But I was lucky. Early one morning as I was passing some large country houses quite a long way before the town, I read, cut in the stone gate-post of one of them, the words *Villa Frankenstein*. I had arrived.

'I spent the next four days in the woods above the house, waiting for you to come walking that way, so that I could speak to you. But you never came. Instead, one afternoon I saw a young woman with a child coming up the path. I did not know who this child was. But as I watched him picking flowers and wandering nearer and nearer the place where I lay, an idea came to me. I would try human company once more. If I could take a child like this, too young to have fixed ideas, it might grow up to love me and be my friend. Yes, I would carry him off to some lonely place in the mountains and bring him up in my way.

'So I waited until the child came into the wood, and then got hold of him. He fought and cried out. The young woman came up and tried to pull him away. I held the child out of her reach; but I was holding him by the neck, and by the time I had dealt with her he was dead.

'I knew I could not stay after that, and so I crossed the mountains to this place, where I have been living in a cave on the edge of the glacier ever since. I was going to come to you, because I have something to ask you.

Instead, you have come to me!

'Yes, Frankenstein, with the strength that you gave me I could kill you now, and your friend as well. But because I need you, I will not. I need you to make my miserable life worth living. Make me happy and I will be good?

At this, Frankenstein, who had remained silent all through the Monster's story, began to show interest. 'What do you want?' he asked.

'A wife,' the Monster replied.

'A wife?' cried Frankenstein. 'Are you mad? Where can I find a woman who would want to be the wife of an evil creature like you?'

'You cannot find one,' said the Monster. 'That is why I have come to you. You must make me one.'

'What!' shouted Frankenstein. 'Make another like you?'

'A woman — as ugly as myself.'

'Never!' said Frankenstein. 'The very idea is so frightful that I will not even think of it. Even if you throw me down the deepest crack in the ice I will never make another like you.'

The Monster smiled again his evil smile. 'Even if I throw not only you, but all those whom you love down with you? Master, think again. You are putting others in unnecessary danger— your friend here, your father, the young woman who lives in your house. Besides, I am ready to make you a promise. As soon as you have made her we will both leave the world of cities and men, and go to the forests of South America. You will never see or hear from us again.'

For a time nobody spoke. Then Frankenstein turned to me. 'Leave us, Henri,' he said. 'Go back over the ice and wait for me there. This creature must have an answer.'

I wanted to stay, but I could see from Frankenstein's look that he wanted to be left alone. The sun had already gone behind the mountain, and a cold wind began to blow down the glacier.

'Come soon,' I said, and started back across the ice. When I looked back they were as I had left them, still talking on the rock while their shadows grew longer.

Chapter Fourteen

It was an hour before I saw Frankenstein coming back across the glacier. If he had been any later he would have been in danger of losing his way among the cracks. But for the Monster to let him go at all must mean that they had reached an understanding of some kind. He came on so slowly that I could tell what that understanding was. It was not just because he was tired: he brought news that he was unwilling to tell.

'Did you promise?' I asked.

'How could I not have promised? He calls me "master", but he knows very well who commands and who obeys.'

'And if they have children?' I asked. 'If they create a new race in South America, enemies of the human race...?'

'I cannot even be sure that he will keep his promise and go to South America,' Frankenstein replied. 'But that is a chance I have to take. What can I do, Henri? He comes and goes so secretly. His powers are more than human. He will destroy my family if I do not do what he wants. God knows how hateful this is to me, but I cannot do anything else. I just have to make another monster. And...', he stopped, as if uncertain how to go on. 'And again I shall need your help. Are you willing to give it?'

This was the question I feared. I had done little to help with the first monster. That had been Frankenstein's creation. Would the second monster be not just his, but ours? I did not think it right to make a second one. And yet, if I did not help, and the second monster was not made, I would be leaving the Frankensteins to face certain death. Also, even after all that had happened, I had to be fair to the Monster. Did he not have a right to happiness? Those words of his kept coming back to me: 'Make me happy and I will be good?' The mistake had been to make the first monster; but having made it, might Frankenstein not be right to make another?

'I will help you,' I said at last, 'but only by keeping you supplied with what you need, by keeping you fed, and by carrying letters to and from the place where you work. But I will take no part in the work itself.'

'I ask no more,' said Frankenstein in reply.

We returned to Belrive the next day. The weather remained fine, and we began once more to live that happy family life which we had almost forgotten. The deaths of Justine and William were still in our minds, but they no longer hung over us like dark clouds. As for Frankenstein's promise to the Monster, he seemed to put it quite out of his mind for the next few weeks. Time passed pleasantly. We went out in the boat, we read in the garden, we went for walks in the hills. We did everything rather than begin work on the new monster. In fact, Frankenstein found so many reasons for waiting that I began to wonder if he would ever begin.

In the end two things moved him to start. First his father called him into his room one day.

'Victor,' he said, 'you will remember that just before your mother died she told you her greatest wish. I am an old man, and it would please me if before I died I could

see that wish come true. It may be that by now you think of Elizabeth more as a sister than as a possible wife. You may even know someone else whom you like better. If so, you must say, because I am not the kind of father who forces his children to marry against their will. Please think about this: if she is not to marry you, we must find somebody else for her. She has a right to know what your feelings are.'

Frankenstein knew that his father was right. Elizabeth ought to know how she stood. She had never said a word about marriage, or even let him feel that she was thinking of it. About his own feelings he was quite clear. Yes, he wanted to marry her — he had had no doubts about it since the death of Justine — but not yet. First he had to carry out his promise to the Monster.

This was one thing that made him decide to begin work. But there was another. Elizabeth was not just a simple housekeeper. She had a quick mind and a woman's natural curiosity. She knew that Frankenstein's unhappiness was not the result of William's and Justine's deaths alone. Something else was troubling him, and she wanted to know what it was. Nor was this just curiosity. She loved my friend, and only wished to learn his secret in order to help him.

However, both Victor and I had always been careful to keep the truth from her, We thought it would do her no good to know; and we did not like it when a most unpleasant happening one night gave her much to think about.

At this time we used to go to bed quite early. There was nothing to stay out of bed for in the country. Besides, Frankenstein did not find it easy to talk to his father and Elizabeth. He had too much to hide, too much that he could only talk about to me. So, one windless, moonless night, a few days after old Frankenstein's talk

with his son, Elizabeth lay in bed reading by the light of a candle. Opposite her was the dark square of the open window; and through it from time to time little flying things kept coming in, drawn by the light of her candle.

She looked up from her book as one of them flew in, and her eye was caught by the appearance of the window. There was something different about its shape — something that had not been there before. She looked again. Two large, brown, hairy hands had appeared at the bottom of the window. As she watched, too frightened to move or speak, the hands turned white as their owner slowly pulled himself up.

Elizabeth was prepared for the face of a thief, but not for this; not for the hanging yellow skin, the watery eyes, the knotted hair and the join lines. She let out a sharp cry, and the face dropped below the window again. The hands disappeared. Less than a minute later I was in her room and listening to her story.

I lit a lamp and went out into the garden. I hurriedly kicked soil over the marks of feet that I found in the soft earth of the flower-bed below Elizabeth's window. '. . . a dream, a bad dream . . .' I could hear Frankenstein saying in the room above.

'I tell you again, it was not a dream, Victor,' Elizabeth replied, coming to the window. 'Can you see anything down there, Henri?'

'Nothing,' I said truthfully. I said nothing about what I *had* seen.

'See,' said Frankenstein. 'How could anyone put his hands on your window and pull himself up, as you said? It is more than three metres to the ground. Why, a man would have to be unnaturally tall to do such a thing.'

Elizabeth said no more. She knew we were trying to hide something, but it was not her way to ask questions.

She shut the window, and went back to bed.

Next morning Frankenstein came to my room with the look on his face of a man who has decided on action.

'I cannot leave things any longer,' he said. 'The creature has been watching us for weeks. Last night he must have been trying to find me and went to the wrong window. I know he will not let me alone until I have done what he wants. I cannot take the chance of another visit like last night's. Besides, who knows? Next time it could really be Elizabeth whom he has come to see. I cannot have her frightened like this. We start work at once.'

'But you cannot work here,' I said. 'She already knows that something is going on.'

'Exactly. That is why I am going to leave home. In my search for the Monster earlier this year I found by chance an empty wood-cutter's hut in the valley of the Arve. It is far enough from Belrive to make it safe from family visitors, but near enough to Geneva for me to get the supplies I need.'

'And my job?' I asked.

'It will be better if you stay here most of the time,' he replied. 'But you will visit me often, bringing food and letters.' He stopped and thought for a minute. 'There is another thing I want you to do...'

I looked at him expectantly.

'If, for any reason, I fail to complete this work, it may not be me who will suffer first, but Elizabeth. Guard her, and be prepared for anything.'

Chapter Fifteen

The first thing that Frankenstein did after breakfast that day was to take Elizabeth off into a quiet corner of the garden, where he asked her to marry him. She did not

say no, and they returned smiling to the house. As
I shook my friend's hand and kissed Elizabeth, I felt
happy in their happiness, but at the same time a little
sad. We three had been friends for so long. Although
marriage would join two of us more closely, it was
certain to separate them from the third. To tell the truth,
I was more than a little in love with Elizabeth myself.

However, this was no time for thoughts of love. After
naming a day in November for their marriage,
Frankenstein went on to talk about his present plans.

'Father,' he said, 'you will be pleased to hear that
I have decided to take up my scientific studies again—at
least, for a time. For this I need peace and quiet, and to
be free from anything, or anyone'—he smiled at
Elizabeth—'who might take my mind off my work.
Therefore I am going to move into a hut in the valley of
the Arve, where I can carry out my experiments.'

'Am I not going to see you at all, then?' asked
Elizabeth.

'It will only be for two months.'

'Two months!'

'You will miss nothing by not seeing him,' I said.
'I know what he is like when he is working. He can
think of nothing but his experiments.'

'And you can write to me, of course,' Frankenstein
went on. 'Henri will visit me often to bring me food and
other things. He can bring your letters, too.'

'And bring back your letters, if you have time to
write them,' Elizabeth replied. She smiled, but it was
clear that she felt hurt and unwanted.

Old Frankenstein was glad that the marriage he so
much wanted had been fixed at last; and glad, too, that
his son had decided to take up work again. He did not
like to see him wandering unhappily and, as it seemed to
him, pointlessly around the countryside. Although he

was sorry that he could not carry out his studies at home, he raised no difficulties about his son's going.

Elizabeth, on the other hand, knew that we were not telling the whole truth, and this hurt her even more. She had kept her doubts to herself after the face had appeared at the window, and she did the same now. But I could see that she did not like someone asking to marry her one minute and telling her untrue stories the next.

We spent the rest of that day putting Frankenstein's scientific instruments in boxes; also all the things he would need for living in the hut. These were then loaded up, and early the next morning we set off for the valley of the Arve.

It was a silent journey. Frankenstein seemed deep in thought for most of the time. As for myself, I was happy simply to enjoy the beauty of the late summer weather, and the hours passed quickly.

The hut was well chosen. Surrounded by trees, and well away from the road up the valley, it was not a place where anybody might by chance call in. A fast-flowing stream ran nearby, which joined the grey waters of the Arve a little lower down.

Here Frankenstein settled in, and after receiving more loads of supplies from Geneva, he began work. By 'supplies' I mean for the most part scientific supplies, glass pipes and containers, wires, burners etc. But there was another kind of 'supplies' which was not to be bought from Geneva merchants. Frankenstein used to give me letters which I took to men living in the poorer parts of the town who, if they were not really thieves, certainly had the manner and appearance of thieves.

These letters were only the orders. It was calling for these orders later that I found far worse.

'It will be better if you call at night,' Frankenstein used to say. 'There will be fewer people in the streets to

ask questions.'

Questions might well have been asked about these carefully tied-up objects, sometimes about two metres long, and heavy. If I had been stopped and searched I might have found it hard to find answers. However, I did what he asked me to do; and when I reached the hut I always helped him to carry these objects inside. While he dealt with them I used to go for a walk in the woods. I hardly went into his work-room at all. The smell was not pleasant, and there was too much there that I did not want to see.

The work went on through September and into October. As time went on, Frankenstein needed fewer supplies, so I spent more time at Belrive, which was where I would rather be. However, there were difficulties to face even there. The trouble was that Elizabeth had begun to ask questions about Frankenstein's work, and I could not escape them. I did not want to tell her lies. Neither could I tell her the exact truth.

'Why don't you take me to the cottage the next time you go, Henri?' she used to say. 'It would be a nice surprise for him.'

'My dear Elizabeth, I've told you before. The journey is long and tiring, and you know very well that Victor would not get any work done while you were there. He is very busy.'

'I wish you'd tell me what this work is.'

'I'm not a scientist like Victor,' I used to reply rather weakly. 'I don't know what it is about.'

'Henri, you do, but you won't tell me. Oh, how can you do this to me? And we have been friends for so long.'

This kind of talk happened about once a week, and although I knew Elizabeth was not quite serious, and only did it to make fun of me, she really was curious, and it was only natural that she should be.

I did once put forward the idea to Frankenstein that we should tell her everything. The three of us had lived so much of our lives with no secrets from each other. It seemed wrong to be hiding the truth from her now. But he would not listen when I spoke of it, and I had to go on as before.

There was one thing, though, which really made me glad to stay at Belrive. I simply did not like being at the hut, least of all at night. The trees came too close, the rooms were dark, and there was such a feeling of being alone.

But that was not all. I may have felt alone in one way, but not in another. While Frankenstein was working, I often went and sat by the stream reading a book. It was at times like these that I felt I was being watched. It was not that I ever saw the watcher, though sometimes I might see the leaves of a bush move when there was no wind; or hear the sound of dead wood breaking beneath the weight of an unseen foot. But the watcher was there all the time, and I could never quite forget him. I did not speak of this to Frankenstein; I did not think it was necessary. He knew as well as I that the Monster was making quite sure that his work was being done.

In one way I was glad about this. If our enemy was living somewhere near the hut he could not be at Belrive. Elizabeth and old Frankenstein were safe — safe, at least, as long as Frankenstein's work went well. But, as I often asked myself, what did 'well' mean? Was it really doing well to bring another monster into the world of men?

Chapter Sixteen

The work went on. By the end of October the New Woman was complete, and Frankenstein was only

waiting for the right weather to put life into her. I had had nothing to do with my friend's work, and had not even entered his work-room for many weeks. But now he had finished, and to please him I went in to see what he had done. So I found myself looking down on my friend's second creation. There she lay, dreaming of life beneath the clear liquid.

This time Frankenstein had not even tried to give beauty to his creature. 'Make her as ugly as myself,' had been the Monster's words on the glacier. Later to Frankenstein alone he had said why. 'Only such a one will want to live with me.'

The Monster would be pleased to see how well his orders had been carried out. As I looked down at Frankenstein's work I felt sick. With her hairy chest, her short thick legs and her huge feet she was disgusting. He really had made a beast. I thought with horror of love between these creatures, and of the race of monsters that might grow out of this love, each one born to hate the human race.

Although the nature of his work would have sickened most men, Frankenstein had not been unhappy during the past weeks. Hard work was always good for him; but now that he had finished he began to get restless and excited. He went for long walks in the woods and returned tired and silent.

The trouble was the weather. To complete his experiment Frankenstein needed, if not a thunderstorm, at least a thundercloud. But it remained unusually sunny and cloudless for the time of the year. The longer he waited, the more time he had to think; and the more he thought, the more the doubts that seemed to come crowding into his mind.

Nor was Frankenstein the only one to suffer from this waiting. The Monster, too, was becoming more and

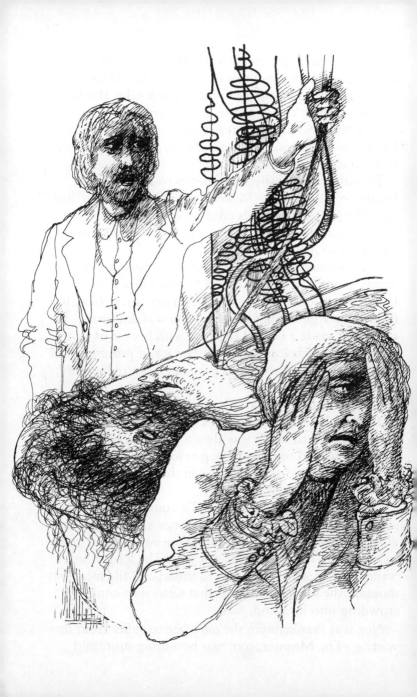

more excited. We first began to notice the marks of his feet very close to the house. Then, as the days passed, his face appeared at the window several times. He did not try to come in; nor did he ever say a word. But he did not have to. His being there made his meaning clear enough.

I stayed in the hut for five days after the completion of the body. But as the fine weather seemed as if it would go on for some time yet, Frankenstein thought I might as well go back to Belrive.

'I shall watch the weather, and return at once if storm clouds appear,' I told him. 'Do not try to finish the work by yourself. You will need me if things go wrong.'

'Nothing is going to go wrong. I know exactly what I have to do,' he said in a voice that seemed to carry hidden meanings.

I had the feeling as I left him that day that something was wrong.

I stayed in Belrive for two days. This time, rather to my surprise, Elizabeth said very little about Frankenstein and the hut. She seemed to have a lot to do in the house, and as I also had things to do, we spoke very little. The weather remained much the same, but I thought I had better not be away from the hut too long, and on the morning of the third day I set off again. However, old Frankenstein had some business he wanted me to do for him in Geneva, so I went into the town on my way.

I had just passed through the town gates when I met an old friend.

'Why, Clerval,' he said, 'what ever has your friend Frankenstein been doing? The whole town is talking about it, and some say . . .' He looked around him before continuing in a quieter voice, '. . . that you are mixed up in it, too. As an old friend, I cannot believe it of you, or

of Frankenstein either. But be careful. It might be safer not to be seen in Geneva just now.'

I stood there staring in surprise. 'Is this some joke?' I asked. 'What ever are you talking about?'

'Do you mean to say,' he said, 'that you do not know that Frankenstein is in prison?'

'In prison?' I said like a fool. 'What for? What has he done?'

'Why, he killed someone, they say. If you really haven't heard the news, let me tell you. It all began two days ago when a boy fishing on the banks of the Arve — about a kilometre above the place where it flows into the Rhône — found something caught in the branches of a tree that was growing out into the water. He pulled it out and found it was a human leg!

'Of course, he went and told the authorities, and people came down to look at it. But there was no doubt about it. It was indeed a human leg.'

'What happened next?' I asked. I still could not think what had gone on at the hut after I had left.

'Why, they searched both banks of the Arve right up to where Geneva ends and Savoy begins, to see if they could find anything else. But there was nothing. Had the leg come from higher up the river in Savoy? If so, there was nothing our Geneva people could do about it. But then they decided to look up some of the streams that flow into the Arve, and in one of them, this time caught between some rocks, they found the upper part of a human arm. A little further up was a wood-cutter's hut, and there they found Frankenstein getting ready to leave.

'Nor was that all. They also found an axe with dried blood on it. They say he must have killed someone, cut the body into pieces, and thrown them into the stream. What do you think about all that?'

At first I could not think at all. My mind would not work. But it did not take me long to see that I had to get out of Geneva quickly. I could not help Frankenstein if I was in prison, too. Besides, his father had to be told. So I hurriedly said goodbye to my friend, and turned my horse back along the road to Belrive.

Questions raced around my brain. And by the time I had got to Cologny, half-way to Belrive, I had found answers to most of them. Yes, it must have happened like that. When I left Frankenstein at the hut, he was clearly having doubts about the whole experiment. If he had been able to give life to his new monster as soon as he had finished her, he would have done so without further thought. But he had had to wait. He had time to change his ideas. He had decided not to give life to yet another monster, with all the dangers that this might have for the human race.

So having waited for a time when the Monster was away — perhaps he had even succeeded in sending him away — he had pulled the body out of the bath, and, after cutting it into pieces with the axe, had thrown it into the stream. Perhaps it was lucky that those two pieces had been found. If Frankenstein had not been taken to prison the Monster would surely have found out what he had done. In his madness he would have killed him then and there. At least he was safe in prison.

But with this last thought came another. If Frankenstein was safe, Elizabeth and his father were not. Indeed, they were in the greatest danger. At once I began to drive my horse on faster. I had to get back to Belrive as quickly as I could. It might even be too late already!

Chapter Seventeen

When I reached the house I jumped off my horse, and did not even stop to tie it to the usual tree before running inside. By then I felt sure that something frightful had already happened. But as I entered the sitting room, what did I see? Old Frankenstein sitting in his favourite window-seat quietly reading a book. So the Monster had not reached the house, after all. There was still time to prepare.

In as few words as possible I told the old gentleman about Victor being in prison. He had already suffered so much, and for a minute I feared that this bad news would make him ill. However, he seemed to take it in without too much excitement, and I went on:

'Victor, of course, has not killed anybody. They have made a mistake, and can prove nothing in a court of law. You will do what you can to get him out of prison. But this is not all. There is danger. I cannot tell you now what Victor has been doing. All I will say is that he has made an enemy — a powerful bloodthirsty enemy who, if he cannot destroy Victor himself, will destroy his family and friends. We must prepare ourselves for his coming; he may even be here tonight. Elizabeth must be told at once.'

'Ah, my friend,' said the old man, shaking his head sadly. 'You have come too late. Elizabeth is not here.'

'Not here?' Now it was my turn to be surprised. 'Where is she, then?'

'Just after you left this morning she told me that she was going to visit Victor in his hut. She went off with our servant, Emile, at about nine o'clock.'

No wonder she had been so quiet about Frankenstein and the hut! She had been planning this journey all the time. She knew that I would not take her, so she had

decided to go by herself—to the hut of all places, where it was very possible that the angry Monster was waiting. I had expected the Monster to come to Elizabeth, but I had never expected Elizabeth to go to him.

There was no time to waste. While old Frankenstein got ready to go to Geneva to try to get his son out of prison, I took a fresh horse and rode back along the lake. This time I took a pistol with me. From now on it was kill or be killed.

I left the lake road at Cologny, and followed small country roads to the valley of the Arve. There was just a chance that I might meet the Monster on the way, since he would not go by the busy road that Elizabeth had taken. There was still a chance that he had missed her; still a chance that she would not find the hut.

However, I did not meet the Monster on the way. And when I came at last to the edge of the wood in which the hut stood, my fears increased. Two untied horses were eating the grass. These were the horses that Elizabeth and Emile had taken. Emile would never have left them to wander like this.

I tied my own horse to a tree and went the rest of the way on foot, holding my pistol ready. As I came near the hut I stopped and listened, but there was no sound except the noise of the stream. Stepping forward, I looked in through the open window of Frankenstein's work-room.

Everything in it had been completely destroyed! Only a creature of more than human strength and more than human hate could have done such things as had been done in that room: every piece of metal bent and torn; every piece of wood broken into the smallest pieces; glass beaten to powder. Only a madman could have done it, and I tried not to think of what the angry Monster might do to a living person if this was what he

did to things.

I went in and searched every room of the hut, but found nobody, dead or alive. I looked all round the outside of the hut, but still found nothing.

At first I did not see Emile lying by the side of the stream. It was not exactly that I did not see him. I just did not see him as a human shape. His arms, legs and head were so unnaturally arranged that he looked like something else. Every bone in his body must have been broken. I could see at once that he was dead, but what about Elizabeth? I went up and down the stream several times and found nothing. I searched the woods near the hut. Still nothing.

I spent the rest of the afternoon looking in ever-widening circles round the hut without any success. Then, just before it began to get dark, beside a path leading out of the wood on the south I found a shoe. It was Elizabeth's. With fear in my heart I searched all round this place but found nothing else. To find nothing was best, I told myself. He must surely have carried her off alive.

Just as this thought came into my mind I heard a sound behind me. I reached for my pistol, but there was no need.

'Frankenstein!' I cried.

'Have I come too late?' he asked. Then as he saw doubt in my face, he said: 'Don't be afraid. I haven't escaped. My father promised to bring me in front of the judges when the time comes, and they let me out. I don't have to tell you what happened after you left me. You know my mind. You must know what I did here. Now you must tell me what has happened here since.'

I told my story, short as it was. When I had finished, he took the shoe from me and held it close to his heart for a long time without speaking. He looked like an

unhappy child holding on to a favourite plaything. He seemed to have lost all power to do anything.

I led the way back to the hut. It was now dark and cold. I made a fire with the bits of broken furniture and we ate the small amount of food that I had brought along. What were we to do? The trouble was that we knew nothing. Was Elizabeth alive or was she no more than a broken body lying in some dark corner of the woods? We did not know. But the hope that she was alive remained. If the Monster had meant to kill her he would surely have done it here. He must have taken her with him, either as a way of making Frankenstein begin work again on a new body, or to make her his wife. The great question was where had they gone, and to that there seemed to be no answer.

In the end we cleared a corner of the room and settled down for the night. We could do nothing until the first light of day. Perhaps even then we could do nothing.

Chapter Eighteen

We were tired, but we did not sleep. As well as the unanswerable questions that raced around our minds all night the sound of thunder far away wakened old fears. The fine weather which had been the cause of Frankenstein's deciding to end the experiment was breaking up at last.

Cold and hungry, and with arms and legs that did not seem to want to bend, we went out at first light and led our horses to drink from the stream. Then we started along the path where I had found the shoe the day before. All we knew was that the Monster had passed that way about sixteen hours earlier. He could be anywhere by now.

We stopped and thought, and decided to continue

along the path. We had no better ideas. We followed it out of the woods to the south-west until we came to a place where it went two ways. One way turned back towards the upper Arve valley, and the other continued towards the Salève. Had he gone up the Arve to Chamonix and the great glacier above? It made sense. He knew we could never follow him through the snows of the highest mountains at this time of the year.

As we stopped there, trying to decide which path to take, I noticed something lying a little way along the second of the two paths. I got down from my horse and walked over to pick it up. It was Elizabeth's other shoe! Frankenstein came up, took it in his hands and turned it over doubtfully.

'Well,' I said, 'aren't you pleased? Isn't it a piece of luck? Just when we need to know which way they went, we find this.'

'Exactly,' my friend replied. 'Just when we need to know. Luck? I'm not so sure.'

'Then it must be Elizabeth's doing,' I said. 'She's trying to show us the way.'

Frankenstein shook his head. 'I think the truth is less simple than you think, I believe both these shoes were dropped by the Monster.'

'By the Monster?' I cried. 'But why should he want us to know where he has gone?'

'Don't you see? To draw us into his power,' was Frankenstein's answer. 'I think he wants to destroy all three of us. He has Elizabeth, and he is using her to catch us. That shoe was lying right in the middle of the path. It was just too easy.'

I did not believe him then. But when at the next place where the path went two ways we found a handkerchief hanging from a branch of a tree, I began to think my friend might be right. I kept my hand on my pistol from

that time on.

It was about ten o'clock when we stopped to rest under the shadow of the Salève. It was not clear where we were meant to go from there. If the Monster was looking for a wild place to live in, he would not choose the Salève. This was not a place of snow and ice, but pleasant grassland lying on top of great white cliffs.

Frankenstein had said little that morning; but there was a look on his face that told me more than words could ever tell. He would not rest now until he had destroyed his creature — or until he was himself destroyed.

More thunder sounded, much nearer now. I looked up to the mountain, now unusually clear in the still, heavy air that waited for the coming storm. Something was moving along the edge of the cliff. 'Too big for a man, or an animal,' I said, pointing.

Frankenstein looked up. 'But not for a monster carrying a girl,' he said. 'You see, he is right on the edge of the cliff where he can be seen against the sky. Clever. He knows we are here, and means us to follow him.'

We rode on towards a break in the cliff, where it was possible to climb up to the top by a rocky path. There we left our horses and started climbing. Usually the Monster would have been able to move much faster than us, but even he must have felt the weight of Elizabeth, and when we got to the top we found ourselves not so far behind him.

'If he saw us when we were below, why did he not attack us when we were coming up the cliff? Why is he racing on like this?'

'He still wants to lead us on,' Frankenstein replied. 'He is making for the highest point of the cliff. When he gets there he will throw her down. And if we are there to see him do it, the greater will be his pleasure.'

The storm was about to break over us. As we pushed
on higher and higher over the rough grass, the first few
heavy drops of rain began to fall. Every few minutes a
flash of lightning lit up the shape of the Monster, half
carrying, half pulling Elizabeth nearer and nearer to the
place he had chosen for her death. He was tired now,
and as we began to get closer, he kept looking back.
Evil burned in his eyes, and his hair made wet by the
now heavy rain hung down over his face like oily rope
ends.

Frankenstein and I were climbing side by side. Since
I was on the cliff side, I gave as much attention to the
placing of my feet as to what the Monster was doing.
One careless step on the wet rock meant a fall of a
hundred metres and certain death.

We were very close behind him when the first
lightning struck the high rocks in front. I remember
smelling that strange burning smell that it gives off when
close. The Monster stopped, and I thought at first that he
was blinded by the flash. But then he suddenly turned to
face us, holding Elizabeth in his arms.

I pulled out my pistol from inside my coat where
I had been keeping it dry. I just had time to see that
I could not possibly use it without putting Elizabeth in
danger, when all at once the Monster raised her high
above his head and threw her at me with all his strength.

If her body had struck me any higher, it would have
carried me over the edge; which, of course, was what
the Monster was trying to do. As it happened, only my
feet went over, and I found myself hanging there with
my arms around Elizabeth's neck. She put her arms
round my neck, and there we were, both for the minute
helpless; she lying on the edge, and me hanging over it.
I remember listening to the sound of my pistol falling
from rock to rock, until at last it went off with a loud

noise somewhere near the bottom of the cliff.

'Hold on! Hold on!' I cried, wildly trying to find a
foothold in the rock. I could not see what Frankenstein
and the Monster were doing. Nor did I care. The most
important thing in the world for me just then was to get
one leg over the edge of the cliff. I did it. After that it
was not hard to get my whole body up. As I lay there
getting my strength back, I saw that Frankenstein and
the Monster were fighting further along on the edge of
the cliff. The rock beneath their feet was wet with the
blood that poured from a wound in the Monster's chest.
It had been made by a knife in Frankenstein's hand.
However, the Monster's own huge hand had closed over
his, and with a sudden movement the Monster tore the
knife from him. He raised it high above his head. For the
first time I saw real joy on his face. I turned my head
away. I could not see my friend die.

There was a blue flash, and then I could see nothing.

I woke up to pain and the smell of burning. This time it
was not just the smell of burnt air. My coat was on fire.
I tore it off, threw it on the ground and put the fire out
with my feet. One side of my face hurt, and as I put my
hand up to feel it, I found that some of my hair was
burnt. All round me the grass was brown and smoking.
I had stood closer to death than I had ever stood before,
and I thanked God that I was still alive.

Elizabeth was lying at my feet. Her clothes were also
burnt, but the heavy rain had already put out the fire.
I raised her to her knees, and as I held her body to mine
I felt her heart beating. She was alive.

But what about Frankenstein and the Monster?

I turned to where I had last seen them. One blackened
mass was all that was left of their bodies. Together in
death, creator and creature could no longer be separated.

It was some time before I could work out what had happened. The knife which the Monster had raised to drive into Frankenstein's body had drawn down the lightning upon him. That same force of nature which had created him had destroyed him.

Shaking myself free from the waking dream that held me, I pulled Elizabeth to her feet, and hand in hand we hurried down the mountain, not stopping until we reached the frightened horses below.

Blackened, burnt and wet to the skin, we rode to Geneva in complete silence.

Afterwards

For some, at least, this strange, unhappy story ended well. Although we did not know it, as we rode through the rain that day, happier days were waiting for Elizabeth and me.

The death of Victor was a heavy loss to bear, whether he was remembered as a friend, or a lover or a son. Old Frankenstein took the news badly, as one might expect. But he was strong in mind and body. He lived not only long enough to give Elizabeth and me his blessing when we got married, but also to see our first son given the name of Victor.

I am an old man now—as old as Frankenstein's father was then. Like him, too, I have lived to see the death of a much-loved wife. Since it cannot be long before I follow her, I have set this story down, as I promised at the beginning, so that it will not die with me.

As for the secret of creating life, that died with Frankenstein. Perhaps, as scientists learn more, that secret will one day be rediscovered. But by that time I shall be dead. And I think I shall not be sorry.

List of extra words

authorities *people who rule*

brain *the mind; grey matter inside the head*

chains

cliff

cracks *lines caused by breaking*

creature *a living person or thing*

disgusting *very nasty, making one feel sick*

experiment *a scientist's work, finding the result of doing certain things*

flash *a sudden bright light*

French *of France*

glacier *a slow-moving river of ice*

horror *a feeling of great fear*

however *but*

human *of men, women, or children*

kite

lightning

monster *a very large, strange and frightening animal or person*

murder *break the law by killing a person*

pistol

thunder *the sound of an electric storm*

university *a place of higher learning*

wire *a metal line that electricity can travel along*

Longman Group Limited
London

Associated companies, branches and representatives
throughout the world

This edition © Longman Group Ltd 1978

First published 1978

ISBN 0 582 52546 2

Set in Bembo 12/13pt.
Printed in Hong Kong by
Sheck Wah Tong Printing Press Ltd.